CW01497749

Original title:
Citrus Clamps Beneath the Mermaid Yawn

Copyright © 2025 Swan Charm
All rights reserved.

Author: Olivia Oja
ISBN HARDBACK: 978-1-80563-167-5
ISBN PAPERBACK: 978-1-80564-688-4

Shimmering Citrus in Mermaid's Hands

In the twilight glow of sea's embrace,
Mermaids dance with a citrus grace.
Golden orbs in their gentle hands,
Sparkling wonders from vibrant lands.

Beneath the waves where secrets dwell,
Echoes of laughter, a sweet, soft spell.
Juicy treasures from ocean's heart,
Each burst of flavor, a work of art.

Tides of Tang and Treasure

Waves roll in with a tangy spray,
Golden fruits in the light of day.
Pirates' dreams on this sunlit shore,
Citrus spills like a treasure trove's roar.

Castles rise from the salty sweep,
Hidden riches in the ocean deep.
Mermaids sing of their fragrant finds,
Legends of fruits that the ocean binds.

Seafoam and Citrusy Delights

Amidst the foam where the sea winds play,
Lemons and limes greet the break of day.
Sparkling droplets on scales so fine,
Citrus twirls in a dance divine.

Waves paint tales with a zesty flair,
Crimson sunsets and salty air.
Happiness found in sun-kissed tides,
Where citrus dreams and the sea abides.

Lost Citrus Requiem in the Depths

In the depths where shadows creep,
Lies a sorrow the ocean keeps.
Citrus fruits that have lost their glow,
Whispering secrets only the deep can know.

A requiem sung to the fading light,
Echoes of joy in the endless night.
Golden memories of days gone by,
Citrus relics beneath the sky.

Sun-kissed Symphonies of the Deep

The sun dips low, a golden hue,
Its rays dance softly on waters blue.
Whispers of waves, a gentle tune,
Where secrets linger, 'neath the moon.

With each rise and fall, they embrace the shore,
Creating melodies, forevermore.
A chorus of dolphins, bold and free,
In the heart of the depths, they sway with glee.

A singer's heart, it swells with pride,
For in these waters, the dreams abide.
With hints of laughter, joy, and grace,
In sun-kissed symphonies, we find our place.

Fruitful Dreams Beneath the Tides

Beneath the waves, in shadows deep,
Lie dreams of fruits, in silence they sleep.
Juicy whispers, soft and sweet,
Nurtured by currents, they lay at our feet.

Coral gardens, a vibrant scene,
Where wishes bloom, and hopes convene.
Anemones dance, in colors bright,
Painting the depths with pure delight.

Golden shells, treasures to find,
Crafting connections, hearts intertwined.
Beneath the tides, where magic gleams,
Awakened are we, by fruitful dreams.

Siren's Citrus Bouquet

In citrus groves, where sirens play,
A fragrant breeze will guide the way.
Lemon and lime, their songs entwined,
Their zestful chorus, by waves defined.

Mandarin melodies soft and clear,
Bringing the sun, drawing us near.
Orange blooms, in laughter, they twine,
With every breath, their magic divine.

Through tangled leaves, a shimmer of light,
Siren's bouquet enchants the night.
A blossoming world, ripe with delight,
In each citrus note, our dreams take flight.

The Ocean's Kiss on Ripe Slices

Sliced ripe fruits, a feast of the day,
Bathed in the ocean's soft, salty sway.
Watermelon whispers, beneath the sun,
Refreshing bites, where joy's begun.

Pineapple tang, so bright and bold,
Tales of summer, longing to be told.
Mango moments, sweet and divine,
In each loving taste, our hearts align.

The ocean's kiss, on every slice,
A dance of flavors, a gift so nice.
In sunlit laughter, our spirits soar,
As we savor life, and ask for more.

Enchantment of the Sea-touched Orchard

Beneath the boughs where whispers play,
The sea's soft breath entwines the sway.
Fruits of gold in morning's glow,
Whispers of secrets only they know.

In twilight's embrace, shadows dance,
Flickering light, a fleeting chance.
The salt-kissed breeze weaves tales anew,
Of dreams that shimmer in the dew.

Laden branches sway and bend,
Telling stories that love will send.
A melody sung by ocean's spine,
In every fruit, a truth divine.

The waves caress the orchard's roots,
With gentle hands, the sea salutes.
Each rising tide, a song of the night,
Where moonlit magic brings forth light.

So here in this enchanted place,
Nature's harmony finds its grace.
In every bite, a world to taste,
The sea-touched orchard, none can waste.

Siren's Flavor: Deeply Rooted

In shadows low, the sirens sing,
With voices sweet, the echoes cling.
Their calls adrift on waves so wide,
Tales of love and danger glide.

Amid the orchard, roots run deep,
Secrets buried, promises to keep.
Fruits that shimmer, bright and bold,
In every bite, a legend told.

From briny depths to branches high,
A dance of life beneath the sky.
Salt and sweetness, a perfect blend,
Where every harvest seeks to mend.

They lure the hearts with secret charms,
The vibrant hues hide ancient harms.
Yet every taste, a tale reborn,
In luscious bites, we are transformed.

So heed the call of orchard's grace,
Where sirens linger and secret trace.
In flavors rich, their spirits dwell,
Deeply rooted, they weave their spell.

Rippled Echoes of Hidden Fruit

Rippled echoes, hidden deep,
In rustling leaves, the forest sleeps.
Soft sighs of wind, a gentle tease,
Awakening hearts with whispered pleas.

Within the grove, a magic stirs,
The hush of night, the fluttering furs.
Every fruit holds a secret song,
In nature's rhythm, where we belong.

Beneath the branches, shadows play,
As twilight drapes the end of day.
The sweetness ripe, a promise found,
In nature's arms, our souls surround.

Each step we take, the ground will sing,
Of lingering fruits that summer brings.
The ripples swirl in twilight's hue,
Hidden flavors, old and new.

So wander close, let silence guide,
To where the echoes gently slide.
In every bite, a memory's kiss,
Among the hidden, find your bliss.

Harmony of Tangerine and Tide

In orchards bright where colors blend,
Tangerines and tides, hand in hand.
Through golden fields, the waters flow,
A dance of citrus, warm and aglow.

With every wave, a tangy burst,
The salty mist, the citrus thirst.
A harmony sweet as summer's dream,
Where sun and surf forever gleam.

As oranges blush in evening light,
Their fragrance mingles, pure delight.
Ripening slowly in warm embrace,
The tide's caress, a softening grace.

Echoes of laughter fill the air,
With every harvest, love we share.
The sun dips low, the day declines,
In tangerine hues, the world aligns.

So gather 'round, dear hearts so true,
In orchard's heart, find joy anew.
With every fruit, a blissful ride,
A harmony of Tangerine and tide.

Aroma of the Abyss: Zestful Tide

In the depths where secrets dwell,
Whispers rise like a muted bell.
Tides that twist through crystal trees,
Dance of salt in the ocean breeze.

Sunlit waves in a vivid play,
Kissing shores at the break of day.
Golden foams in a joyous spree,
Nature's pulse sets the spirit free.

Aromas twine with the salty air,
Laden whispers that tease and dare.
Every splash tells a tale anew,
Stories etched in the ocean's hue.

Beneath the tides, where shadows creep,
Silent secrets in the fathoms deep.
With each wave, a fresh refrain,
Echoes whispering joy and pain.

A zestful tide is a siren's song,
Pulling hearts where they belong.
In every swirl, the mysteries hide,
Heart and soul in the ebbing tide.

Tranquil Grove of Aquatic Echoes

In a grove where the waters gleam,
Ripples shimmer, as if in a dream.
Lush green canopies softly sway,
Guiding thoughts in the light of day.

Fish dart in shadows, brief and bright,
Chasing sunbeams in playful delight.
Gentle whispers through rustling leaves,
Lull the heart; the spirit believes.

Calm embraces the morning bright,
As the moon fades to the soft twilight.
Serenity in each dropping leaf,
Where worries fade, and hearts find relief.

In the echoes of the tranquil stream,
Sashaying lightly on sunlight's beam.
Nature sings to the wanderer's heart,
Inviting peace, a brand new start.

Aquatic whispers, sweet and clear,
Call to souls that wander near.
In this grove, solace is found,
Wrapped in beauty, tightly wound.

Surreal Slices in a Marine Reverie

Beneath the waves where dreamers dive,
Mystic realms seem to come alive.
Surreal sights uncoil and gleam,
Fragments woven from a hidden dream.

Bubbles dance like laughter caught,
In colorful hues and realms of thought.
Echoing songs of the deep within,
A cadence of joy amidst the din.

Coral gardens in radiant hues,
Where the heart finds love in ocean's blues.
Each wave a brushstroke on the shore,
Crafting art from nature's core.

In twilight's grasp, as shadows play,
The ocean holds the night at bay.
Whispers linger, soft and free,
Painting magic in the mystery.

Slices of surreal in a bounding sea,
Embrace each moment, let it be.
In the realm where dreams take flight,
Dance upon the waves, embrace the light.

Citrus Breeze in the Mermaid's Cove

In the cove where the sea meets sky,
Mermaids sing and the breezes sigh.
Citrus scents waft through the air,
A tapestry spun with love and care.

Golden orbs in the sunlit sheen,
Bright against the ocean's green.
With every note, the heart takes wing,
In harmony with the songs they bring.

Glimmers cast by the tide's embrace,
Where laughter dances in blissful grace.
Coastal treasures in the softest light,
Mirthful melodies fill the night.

Beneath the waves in a sacred space,
Stories linger, time can't erase.
With every breath of the citrus breeze,
The spirit finds its sweet release.

In the cove where dreams unfold,
Whispers of magic woven bold.
Mermaids guard the enchanted scroll,
In the citrus breeze, they soothe the soul.

Orange Blossom Echoes at Twilight

In gardens where the twilight gleams,
The orange blossoms weave their dreams.
Whispers soft begin to sway,
As shadows dance and greet the day.

Their scent a lure, so pure, divine,
Each petal kissed by moon's design.
The stars above in silent flight,
Glow softly on this fragrant night.

With every breeze a story told,
Of sunlit days and nights of gold.
These echoes carry through the air,
A magic held in sweet despair.

Among the blooms, the secrets hide,
Of love and laughter, hopes allied.
A twilight's touch, a fleeting song,
In orange hues where dreams belong.

Beneath the sky in playful grace,
Each blossom finds its perfect place.
Together in the dusk they sway,
As echoes softly fade away.

Melodies of Mellow Citrus Currents

In the heart of orchards vast and wide,
Mellow currents of citrus glide.
Sweet notes dance on the summer breeze,
Their laughter floats through rippling trees.

Each fruit a story, vibrant, bright,
A melody that enchants the night.
Lemon and lime in playful spin,
With oranges crafting dreams within.

Golden rays of sunlight spill,
Over hills where time stands still.
The citrus murmurs, soft and clear,
A ballad spun for all to hear.

Among the blooms, where colors thrive,
The very air begins to drive.
With every breath, a pulse alive,
Melodies that weave and strive.

As twilight falls, the tendrils creep,
In citrus land, the secrets keep.
With every note, the heart ignites,
In whispers sweet of summer nights.

Siren's Bounty: Sweet and Sour

By the silken shore where waves do sigh,
Siren's bounty calls as tides reply.
With sweet and sour in their embrace,
They weave enchantments, time and space.

Lush fruit glimmers in the light,
An offering of day and night.
Their flavors dance in harmony,
A treasure found upon the sea.

From ocean depths, where secrets dwell,
A burst of life, an unspoken spell.
Citrus tangs upon the tongue,
With every taste, new tales are sung.

Waves crash gently on the shore,
Each whisper begs for evermore.
In every wave and echo's roll,
The sirens capture heart and soul.

In twilight's gleam, the flavors blend,
Of sweet and sour, they transcend.
A feast of life, a fleeting chase,
In siren's call, we find our place.

Juices of the Forgotten Sea

Beneath the waves where dreams reside,
The forgotten sea holds the tide.
With juices rich and stories deep,
In salted peace, the secrets sleep.

Each drop a vision, bright and bold,
Of ships and treasures, tales of old.
Citrus hues in ocean's core,
A glimpse of life from days of yore.

The brine whispers of journeys past,
As time flows by, a fleeting cast.
In liquid gold, the sunbeams dance,
Awakening the sea's romance.

Where memories in waves unfurl,
And every ripple starts to swirl.
Juices blend, a potion rare,
In ocean's heart, a hidden lair.

As twilight comes to paint the sea,
The forgotten whispers beckon thee.
In every drop, a world reborn,
In juicy tides, new dreams are sworn.

Whispers of Orchard Waves

In the grove where shadows play,
Fruitful branches sway and dance,
Every breeze spins tales anew,
Whispers of an ancient romance.

Beneath the boughs, the secrets lie,
Nature's heartbeat soft and strong,
With every leaf that rustles by,
The orchard sings its timeless song.

Golden suns and silver moons,
Kiss the fruits with gentle light,
While twilight hums its quiet tunes,
Painting dreams in shades of night.

The gardens bloom with vibrant hues,
As laughter floats on fragrant air,
Each petal tells of whispered views,
Of glories past and moments rare.

In the orchard, time stands still,
Each wave a memory, clear as day,
For in this land of soft goodwill,
Life's sweetest truths do softly sway.

Tide Pools and Tangelo Twilight

As day embraces soft night's weave,
The tide pools glimmer, secrets keep,
Among the rocks, where shadows breathe,
Life dances in the depths so deep.

Tangelo skies blend orange and gold,
Painting horizons with dreams untold,
Every wave a story unfolds,
In tide pools, wonders manifold.

The whispers of the ocean's heart,
Call to the creatures, shy and bright,
In each small splash, a form of art,
Mirrors of the starry night.

Under these skies, the world stands still,
A moment captured, pure delight,
With every splash, the sea will thrill,
In twilight's glow, the heart takes flight.

The charm of dusk, a sweet embrace,
Guides wanderers through silky dreams,
As tide pools hide their mystic grace,
In tangelo twilight, all is as it seems.

Coral Fruits under Moonlit Chants

Beneath the stars, coral fruits glow,
Bathed in moonlight's silver beams,
With every whisper, tales do flow,
Of far-off lands and distant dreams.

The breeze brings secrets wrapped in sound,
Where magic ebbs and also flows,
In this enchanted, timeless ground,
Life blooms in ways nobody knows.

Illuminated by the night,
Colors dance on ocean's crest,
As creatures sing with pure delight,
Each note a treasure, nature's best.

Glistening shells and twinkling eyes,
Join in the chorus of the sea,
While coral fruits wear sweet disguise,
As guardians of the mystery.

In moonlit chants, the dreams arise,
With every tide, they stir and play,
A symphony beneath the skies,
In nature's heart, forever stay.

The Aquatic Orchard's Hidden Pulse

In waters deep, the orchard thrives,
With roots that search and branches rise,
Where fish and fruits in harmony,
Craft a world under the tides.

A pulse beats softly, under swells,
The rhythm of the ocean's grace,
In every drop, a secret dwells,
In aquatic realms, time finds its pace.

With every wave, a story told,
Named by currents, sung by sea,
A treasure trove of dreams of old,
In every pulse, life's tapestry.

Coral branches stretch and sway,
As whispers echo through the blue,
In the depths where shadows play,
The orchard thrives on shades anew.

In this quiet, wondrous place,
The heart of nature beats so strong,
Encircled by the sea's embrace,
The aquatic orchard sings its song.

Tangy Reflections at Dusk

The sun dips low, a golden sphere,
Casting shadows, drawing near.
Whispers of citrus fill the air,
As twilight weaves its magic rare.

In the distance, laughter flows,
From where the gentle river goes.
A hint of lime on summer's breeze,
In twilight's glow, the heart finds ease.

Floating lanterns, soft and bright,
Dance upon the waves of night.
The world adorned in orange shade,
A canvas made with dusk displayed.

Reflections twinkle in the stream,
Nature's secrets start to gleam.
With every splash, a story told,
Of tang and time, both bright and bold.

Enchanted Oranges in the Tidal Pool

Beneath the waves, a hidden glow,
Where oranges in the water flow.
With each new tide, they sway and sway,
In pools of magic, bright and gay.

Coral cradles, soft and kind,
The secrets of the sea entwined.
Their zest brings life to every shell,
In whispers, tales of ocean dwell.

Bubbles rise with laughter's cheer,
As crabs and fish swim ever near.
The sunlit dance, a vibrant show,
In tidal pools where wonders grow.

A flick of fin, a splash of light,
Oranges glisten, pure delight.
Where dreams of potion and spell reside,
In watery realms, our hopes abide.

And so we gather by the shore,
To taste the magic, crave for more.
Enchanted fruits, in sunlight's thrall,
In tidal pools, we find it all.

The Mermaid's Secret Orchard

In moonlit dreams beneath the tides,
An orchard waits where magic hides.
With twisting vines and fruits aglow,
The mermaid's grace, a gentle flow.

With every leaf, a tale is spun,
Of whispered wishes, joy begun.
Lemons bright, like stars, they shine,
In this realm where dreams align.

A melody of waves does call,
Inviting all to share the thrall.
Oranges ripe upon the bough,
Unseen treasures, take a bow.

Each fruit a gem, each branch a song,
Where heartbeats and the sea belong.
In twilight's hush, the secrets beam,
In mermaid's orchard, live the dream.

Grapefruit Glow in Aquatic Shadows

In waters deep, a glow appears,
Where grapefruit dreams dissolve our fears.
Silhouettes of mermaids play,
In shadows soft, they drift away.

The ocean's pulse a gentle hum,
As citrus scents to life succumb.
A splash, a dart, they weave and spin,
In aquatic realms, where tales begin.

Beneath the silver, gleaming light,
Grapefruit floats, a lovely sight.
With every wave, a story churns,
Of lovers lost, and wishes yearn.

Veiled in mist, the journey flows,
While coral blooms in vibrant throes.
In twilight's arms, the shadows play,
As grapefruit dreams drift far away.

And there we find, with hearts aglow,
The magic felt in ebb and flow.
In aquatic shadows, hope ignites,
Where grapefruit sings through starry nights.

Juicy Echoes Beneath the Seafoam

Beneath the waves, where secrets lie,
Whispers of dolphins dancing nigh.
Seafoam sparkles, glimmers bright,
Echoing tales of day and night.

Coral gardens, vivid with hues,
Sheltering dreams, as the ocean ruse.
A treasure trove, both wild and free,
Juicy echoes sing to me.

Gentle currents, weaving through sand,
Holding magic, carved by hand.
Each rising tide tells of lore,
Of ancient mariners reaching shore.

In every bubble, stories swirl,
A mermaid's laugh, a sailor's pearl.
The tide's embrace in the fading light,
Unfurls adventures, taking flight.

Beneath the surface, life entwined,
In sea's deep lull, our hearts aligned.
With every wave, I feel the call,
Juicy echoes, enchanting all.

Echoes of Tropical Lullabies

Echoes float on the balmy breeze,
Carried softly among the trees.
Bananarama in vibrant sway,
Tropical lullabies greet the day.

Coconut palms, a gentle sway,
Rustling leaves in a sweet ballet.
Each note lingers, like honeyed sweet,
A serenade where dreams retreat.

Under the stars, where shadows fade,
Bright fireflies dance, a nightly parade.
Crickets hum their soothing tune,
As the world rests beneath the moon.

Whispers of love in the cool night air,
Wrapped in rhythms, tender care.
From ocean depths to skies above,
In echo's arms, we find our love.

Each lullaby, a soft embrace,
Woven with hopes, a sacred space.
In this land where dreams arise,
We sway to echoes, tropical sighs.

The Salty Kiss of Golden Oranges

Golden rays fall on the sandy shore,
The salty kiss of waves implore.
Oranges glisten, ripe and bright,
Underneath the warm sunlight.

The ocean's breeze carries a tune,
Sweet scents waft, afternoon.
A citrus dream as tides embrace,
Sunshine dances, a warm embrace.

Each bite bursts with summer's glow,
Juicy sweetness, time moves slow.
In each morsel, laughter springs,
A taste of joy that summer brings.

Children play with sandy glee,
With oranges shared by the sea.
A picnic spread, bright and fair,
Moments unfold with the salty air.

As twilight descends with splendor's kiss,
Golden oranges, a moment of bliss.
With every wave and setting sun,
Life's sweet chorus has just begun.

A Bounty of Sun and Sea

In a land where sun and sea unite,
A bounty of colors, a pure delight.
Seashells sing on the sandy strand,
Stories of treasures from a distant land.

Crimson sunsets paint the sky,
While seagulls cry, and dolphins fly.
Each grain of sand holds a tale,
Of ships and dreams that set the sail.

Fishing boats sway in rhythmic grace,
Men of the tide, with weathered face.
Their nets cast wide, a hopeful plea,
For nature's gift from sun and sea.

Children gather, hearts so free,
Building castles by the sea.
With laughter bright and spirits high,
They chase the waves as they rush by.

Together we wander along the shore,
Basking in blessings forevermore.
In this haven where love is key,
We find our home, 'neath sun and sea.

Siren's Tangy Embrace

In twilight's soft and fleeting glow,
Siren songs in whispers flow.
With citrus breath that calls the night,
She beckons from the ocean's light.

Her tangy laughter fills the air,
In dreams where none would know despair.
A hint of zest both sweet and bright,
Enticing hearts to join her flight.

With waves that dance like silver thread,
The sea, a realm where many tread.
In every drop, a story sings,
Of love ensnared by ocean's wings.

But tread with care, oh sailor bold,
For sirens keep their secrets cold.
Their embrace, a tempting snare,
Can lead to depths none should prepare.

So chase the echoes of her call,
The rising tide can be your fall.
For in her song is joy embraced,
Yet danger lurks in every taste.

Luminal Citrus under the Moon's Gaze

Beneath the moon, in silvered sheen,
Citrus dreams serve to convene.
With every squirt, a spark ignites,
As glowing fruit reveals our sights.

The luminescent glow, so bright,
Awakens magic in the night.
With laughter sweet like honeyed dew,
We'll dance beneath the stars anew.

In gardens lush, the fruits do sway,
In playful waltz, they steal the day.
Each glimmered drop, a promise made,
To lead us through the evening's shade.

With scents of orange wafting near,
Our hearts entwined, we lose all fear.
For in this realm, where dreams collide,
The moonlight wraps us safe inside.

So let us bask in luminal flare,
In citrus bliss, we find our lair.
With every taste, the night we seize,
As time dissolves with fragrant breeze.

The Forbidden Citrus Garden

Deep in the woods, a secret lies,
Where tangled vines and shadows rise.
A garden lost to time and fate,
With citrus fruits that tempt, elate.

These orbs of sunlight, bright and bold,
Hold tales of magic, true and old.
Yet whispers warn, beware the fruit,
For sweetness hides in bitter root.

Once tasted, souls may find no peace,
An appetite for more won't cease.
In every bite, a curse ensnares,
For treasures sought bring darkest cares.

Yet wanderers, with hearts so sly,
Seek out the grove beneath the sky.
In every hue, a chance to thrive,
But through the dark, few souls survive.

So heed the lore of garden's grace,
For citrus bright can hide a face.
In every zest, a risk to take,
In forbidden fruits, our hearts may break.

Orange Hues in Azure Waters

Beneath the waves, where secrets dwell,
Emerald dreams and orange swell.
A dance of hues in shifting light,
Where sun and sea connect in flight.

The azure depths hold citrus bright,
That paints the ocean with pure delight.
Here fish do play in colors bold,
In waters warm, their tales unfold.

With every splash, a story spreads,
Of coral homes and starry beds.
The orange tones, a beacon bright,
Invite the curious to take flight.

So dive into these vibrant streams,
Where water shimmers like our dreams.
In every wave, an orange hue,
Awaits to wrap around you true.

In azure realms, let spirit soar,
With citrus winds, we'll drift to shore.
For in this blend of blissful glee,
The ocean's heart will set us free.

The Orange Tide's Bountiful Lullaby

The tide whispers softly, night's gentle kiss,
Orange hues mingle, a moment of bliss.
Shells speak in secrets, tales of the sea,
Carried by waves, wild and free.

With each rolling crest, the world fades away,
A lullaby sung by the sea in ballet.
Sand cradles the moon, as stars start to twinkle,
While dreams drift like boats, on the water's gentle dinkle.

The horizon blushes in a warm, golden light,
As shadowed creatures dance, hidden from sight.
In whispers of orange, tales old and new,
Waves write their chapters, a mysterious cue.

So listen closely, under twilight's embrace,
For the tide has a story, a magical place.
In the heart of the ocean, where mysteries guide,
The soul finds rest in the orange tide.

As dawn stretches forth, awaking the shore,
The bountiful lullaby sings forevermore.
Each note holds a promise, a world to explore,
In the dance of the tide, we're forever in store.

Seaside Spritz of Lively Colors

A splash of the sea, a twist of the breeze,
Where sun-kissed waves glide with effortless ease.
Bright corals stand guard, a vibrant display,
In the heart of the ocean, the colors at play.

With each gentle wave, the canvas unfolds,
Brushstrokes of azure, in whispers that scold.
From turquoise to teal, with a flicker and gleam,
The seaside blooms brightly, a painter's sweet dream.

Shells shimmer and dance with a joyful delight,
While seagulls soar high, in their marvelous flight.
The sun dips below, igniting the sky,
As hues swirl together, with a bashful sigh.

In the air, there's magic, a potion divine,
Each droplet of color, a vintage of brine.
The salty fragrance lingers with glee,
As the shoreline unfurls, wild and free.

Oh, the seaside sings, in colors so bright,
A spritz of enchantment, an everlasting light.
With wishes and dreams, such joy it bestows,
In the lively embrace, where the ocean wind blows.

Coral Loquat and Aquamarine

Beneath the great waves, where wonders reside,
Coral blooms flourish, in colors they bide.
Loquat trees whisper with fruit ripe and sweet,
While currents of aquamarine twirl at their feet.

The dance is enchanting, a ballet so rare,
As fish weave through gardens, without a care.
In a world made of magic, where dreams intertwine,
Coral and aquamarine shimmer and shine.

Through depths unknown, the secrets are kept,
In the arms of the currents, time softly swept.
Nature's own tapestry, woven with grace,
Each thread tells a story, a vibrant embrace.

Amongst these bright wonders, the echoes ring clear,
Tales of the ocean, both far and near.
The loquat's sweet scent mingles with time,
As stories of yore flicker like rhyme.

So dive into dreams where colors collide,
Through coral and loquat, the sea's gentle tide.
An aquamarine carpet unfurls in the light,
As magic and wonder take flight in the night.

The Luminescent Grove Below

In the depths of the sea, where sunlight may wane,
Lies a grove of enchantment, a magical plane.
With creatures that glow in a ethereal hue,
The luminescent grove holds wonders anew.

Beneath the dark waves, where shadows entwine,
The whispers of mermaids and fishes combine.
In a dance of the night, with colors that gleam,
Each flicker a promise, a shimmering dream.

The coral trees sway in a moonlit soft glow,
Guardians of secrets only the deep know.
As pulses of light ripple through aqua clear,
A symphony breathed, for the brave to draw near.

Oh, wander with caution through this jeweled abode,
For magic runs deep, on this mystic road.
With every soft breath, the waters ignite,
Revealing the depths in a dance of delight.

So seek out the grove, let your senses unfold,
In the luminescent glow, where stories are told.
Each shimmer a beacon, where dreams intertwine,
In the mystery of oceans, where wonders align.

Tangerine Dreams in Ocean's Embrace

In twilight's glow, the tangerines gleam,
A dance through the waves, a sweet, silent dream.
Whispers of citrus, they float on the air,
Delightful and bright, like a child's tender care.

Beneath the curls of the azure's sway,
Sun-kissed and playful, they beckon the day.
Each fruit, a promise, a sunlit delight,
In the heart of the ocean, where day meets the night.

Sailing through scents of the warm, salty spray,
The sun and the citrus begin their ballet.
With laughter and joy, in this vibrant terrain,
They weave through the waters, a citrus refrain.

We drift on the breeze, the soft ocean sighs,
Tangerine dreams where enchantment lies.
In waves' gentle rhythm, their essence will stay,
Whirling in currents, forever at play.

The Lament of Zesty Echoes

On rocky cliffs where the seagulls cry,
Whispers of zest in the evening sky.
With sorrowful notes, the citrus bemoans,
A tale of the tides and the ocean's soft moans.

A yearning for shores long lost in the mist,
Bright echoes lingering where dreams once kissed.
In shadows of sunset, the fruit's gentle plea,
Calls forth the memories, rich as the sea.

The tangy nostalgia, a bittersweet song,
In the heart of the ocean, where all things belong.
Each wave sings of longing, of laughter, of tears,
In zesty embraces, it dissolves all fears.

The squall of the seas carries tales from afar,
While citrus far rises, like shimmering stars.
A lamentation that haunts every breeze,
In the sigh of the ocean, a longing to please.

Citrus Whispers Beneath the Waves

Beneath the surface, the waters converse,
With citrusy whispers that thrill and immerse.
Each bubble a secret, each foam a delight,
In hidden alcoves where shadows take flight.

The gleam of the orange, the freshness of lime,
Dance like reflections of sweet summer time.
In currents so gentle, their voices combine,
Citrus and ocean, in harmony divine.

The echo of lemons, both sharp and so sweet,
Create symphonies far beneath our feet.
With every soft ripple, their stories unfold,
The wonder of citrus, a treasure retold.

With tides that embrace and caress all around,
They weave through the depths, where magic is found.
In whispers alluring, forever they play,
Citrus dreams cherished beneath the soft sway.

A Siren's Citrus Serenade

Upon the shores where the wild seas roll,
A siren sings sweetly, enkindled with soul.
Her voice, a delight, drifts soft on the air,
In rhythms of citrus, she lures all who dare.

With tangerines glowing, her song is a gold,
Of legends and stories from ages of old.
Each note a reflection of sun on the tide,
Magic of fruits and the ocean's great pride.

In twilight's embrace, her melodies soar,
Entwined with the waves, they sing evermore.
A fragrant serenade draws the lost to her side,
With citrus enchantment, no heart could abide.

Her fruit-laden songs weave through shadows and light,
An inviting allure in the deep of the night.
With laughter and longing, she beckons them near,
In a world kissed by citrus, where none must fear.

Echoes of Juicy Whispers

In glades where secrets softly tread,
Whispers drift like leaves unfed.
The sunlit fruit hangs ripe and round,
Echoes of laughter, sweetly found.

Frolicsome winds weave through the trees,
Carrying tales on a gentle breeze.
Each berry tells a story true,
Of summer days and skies so blue.

Underneath the boughs, we dwell,
In dreams where shades of magic swell.
The sweetest song in twilight's glow,
With juicy whispers, hearts do flow.

Together we steal the evening light,
With voices lifted into night.
A chorus of fruit, so rich and sweet,
In whispers ripe, our sorrows meet.

Bound by secrets only we hold,
In echoes soft, our truths unfold.
The whispers dance, the stories blend,
In juicy realms where dreams transcend.

The Siren's Sweet Concoction

She brews her potions in moonlit seas,
A melody thick with honeyed ease.
With every wave, a spell is cast,
In her cauldron, shadows are amassed.

Her laughter rings, a chime of gold,
With secrets of ages, waiting to be told.
Sweet nectar drips from sails of lore,
Enticing sailors to her shore.

In bubbles swirling, currents swirl,
Each sip a dance, a fragrant whirl.
A taste of mischief, darkly spun,
In the balance of night and sun.

The siren smiles, her eyes aglow,
In every tide, her whispers flow.
With every taste, a fleeting bliss,
Siren's touch, a dangerous kiss.

Beware the lure, the vibrant prize,
For in her depths, the heart soon dies.
Yet still we crave her sweet delight,
The siren's brew, a tempting night.

Siren's Blossom: A Sea of Zing

In coral gardens where sea blooms thrive,
The siren's song brings colors alive.
With petals bright and scents that tease,
A fragrant breath on the ocean breeze.

Her blossoms sway with the ocean's sigh,
Underneath the vast, eternal sky.
In vibrant hues, enchantments twirl,
Inviting hearts to wish and whirl.

Each floral note, a journey sparked,
Into the depths where magic's marked.
With every drop of dew that gleams,
A world awakens, born from dreams.

In the hush of dusk, their beauty calls,
As shadows dance on ancient walls.
A symphony spun from salt and spring,
In siren's blossom, the heart will sing.

Come sip the air, so sweet and bright,
In this sea of zing, there's no end in sight.
For in each bloom, a wish resides,
In siren's charm, where love abides.

Citrus Tropic Beneath the Surface

Where sunbeams shatter on ocean's crest,
Lies a citrus world, a tropical nest.
Sunkissed fruits in dappled shade,
In hidden groves where joy is made.

Each slice reveals a treasure sweet,
With zest to make the dull days fleet.
Lemon and lime in a playful dance,
Their fragrant spirits in a trance.

Underneath the surface, secrets lie,
In every peel, a soft goodbye.
Whispers of sweetness stir the air,
Inviting all with luscious flair.

The bounty thrives where shadows dwell,
In tangy dreams, we weave our spell.
With colors bright and tart delight,
In citrus tropics, hearts take flight.

From orange dusk to lemon dawn,
The zest of life keeps drawing on.
In every bite, an ocean's wave,
Citrus whispers, bold and brave.

Waves of Tangy Verses

In the shimmer of the sea, bright and bold,
Whispers of citrus dreams, tales untold.
Each wave dances with a sweet delight,
Echoing laughter under the moonlight.

Jellyfish glisten, a canvas of hues,
Splashing in rhythms that brighten the blues.
With the sun on the rise, the tide's embrace,
Nature swirls close, in a lively chase.

The salty breeze sings, the gulls take flight,
Upon golden sands, where day meets night.
A symphony brewing, the ocean sways,
As whispers of tangy verses amaze.

Seashells gather, secrets in their round,
In every cresting wave, stories abound.
The horizon glows, kissed by the sun,
In this boundless expanse, we are one.

So let us wander where the waters gleam,
Get lost in currents, chase every dream.
With hearts wide open, let adventures start,
Among waves of tangy verses, feels like art.

Coral Ruins with Zesty Fragrance

Beneath the waves, where colors blend,
Lies a realm of coral, nature's friend.
Zestful fragrances waft from below,
In vibrant gardens, the sea's bright show.

Determined whispers of ancient tales,
Echo through waters, as time prevails.
Treasures forgotten, in layers of sand,
A magic preserved by the ocean's hand.

Glimmering fishes weave in and out,
Dancing through coral, without a doubt.
Zesty scents swirling, the ocean's embrace,
Inviting us deeper, a magical space.

With each rising tide, stories unfold,
Of legendary journeys, bold and gold.
The past and the present, in currents combine,
In coral ruins, where secrets intertwine.

So let us dive, in this fragrant sea,
To discover the wonders that might be.
With hearts set free, we explore the range,
In the coral ruins, we feel the change.

Fantasia of Sun and Sea

Under the canvas of azure skies,
The sun paints visions, where adventure lies.
In golden rays and breezy tunes,
We dance through dreams, under bright moons.

The sea shimmers bright, a magical sight,
With playful waves that twist and unite.
Shells sprawl like stories upon the shore,
Calling us closer, who could ask for more?

Dolphins leap high, with a spirited cheer,
Charting the flows of the ocean near.
In every ripple, a fantasy waits,
Inviting us closer to many fates.

With laughter that mingles in salty air,
A serenade woven with utmost care.
Every heartbeat syncs in life's grand play,
As sun meets the sea at the close of day.

In this vivid realm of wonder and glee,
We lose ourselves in the endless spree.
For life is a journey, a dream to decree,
In the fantasia of sun and sea.

Citrus Chords in the Silent Ocean

In the depths of the deep, where quiet prevails,
Citrus chords ripple, like soft, gentle trails.
A symphony beckons, so sweet and divine,
In the silent ocean, our hearts intertwine.

Softly the waves whisper, secrets so bright,
Carriers of freshness, draped in moonlight.
The world of the sea, a canvas so vast,
With each note of citrus, we're tethered fast.

Stillness surrounds us, the water is calm,
Each breath we take fills us, like a balm.
A harmony drifting on whiffs of the sea,
In silence we find our place to be free.

Journey through currents, each chord a delight,
A melody woven in the softest twilight.
Embraced by the tides, we drift and we sway,
Harmonies linger, come what may.

So let us wander where the music flows,
Into the ocean's hush, where wonder grows.
With citrus-charged whispers, our spirits will soar,
In the silent ocean, forever explore.

Sea-Infused Citrus Melodies

In the tide's gentle song, citrus sways,
The orange sun dips in glowing rays.
Waves whisper secrets to the shore,
While lemon breezes beckon for more.

Bright zest mingles with the sea's salt dance,
Lime laughter echoes, a lively chance.
Together they twirl in a vibrant spree,
Nature's palette, wild and free.

From citrus groves to ocean's embrace,
Joyful aromas fill this enchanted space.
Fragrant tides wash over the sands,
Crafting dreams with delicate hands.

So let the fruits of the sea align,
In harmony bright, a taste divine.
With every wave, a new tale unfolds,
As citrus and ocean weave threads of gold.

Beneath the moon's gaze, the sweetness lies,
Tales of tang and brine softly rise.
In twilight's glow, salt and zest combine,
A melody sung in the warm, still brine.

The Dance of Lemon and Wave

On the edge where land meets foam,
Lemon blossoms find their home.
Dancing lightly in the breeze,
They sway with grace among the trees.

Each wave a partner, strong and bold,
Whirls of gold and silver unfold.
A citrus twist, a splashy show,
With laughter shared where the wild seas go.

Evening brings the sweetest light,
As lemon dreams take flight at night.
Ocean's heart beats strong and clear,
In harmony, the worlds draw near.

Together they paint the tranquil scene,
In shades of yellow, soft and keen.
Crashing waves with zestful grace,
In every drop, the sun's embrace.

So let the citrus tides align,
As nature hums a tune divine.
For in this dance, both loud and pure,
Lemon and wave forever endure.

The Brightness Within the Deep

Beneath the waves, where shadows shy,
Citrus light begins to fly.
Lemon slices glide with glee,
A splash of joy beneath the sea.

Orange globes in the coral's grip,
Tales of citrus on every trip.
The sun-kissed fruits of vibrant hue,
Glow softly in the ocean's blue.

In depths unknown, flavors reside,
Hints of thrill on every tide.
With seaweed friends, they twirl and sway,
A delicious game where they play.

Bright as stars in the midnight hour,
These fruits embody nature's power.
Carving pathways with every pulse,
Filling the depths with zest and impulse.

So dive beneath where wonders gleam,
And savor drops of citrus dream.
For in the deep, warmth never dies,
With lemon beams, the ocean sighs.

Whimsical Citrus Nightfall

As day retreats in golden light,
Citrus dreams take graceful flight.
Lemon moons rise with gentle grace,
Painting wonder on every face.

Kumquat stars twinkle bright and clear,
In the night, their laughter we hear.
Whispers of zest drift on the breeze,
A symphony played among the trees.

Tangerine shadows start to blend,
In twilight's glow, magic ascends.
Citrus fragrances fill the air,
Bind our spirits in joyful care.

The night is rich, like a sweet embrace,
In every twirl, a warm trace.
With every breath, emotions swell,
Where dreams of fruit and ocean dwell.

So let us dance 'neath the zestful sky,
In this whimsical realm, time will fly.
Held by the magic of night's sweet call,
In our hearts, the citrus enthrall.

Splashing Fragrance of Citrus Delights

In gardens bright with sunlit glow,
The citrus trees in wealth bestow,
With lemons, limes, and oranges fair,
Their fragrance dances in the air.

Each ripe fruit holds a tale untold,
Of summer days and nights of gold,
As dew-kissed leaves gleam in the light,
A symphony of zest in flight.

Beneath the boughs, the children play,
Laughing in the warmth of day,
With every splash and joyous cheer,
The magic of the season near.

From citrus jars, the sorrows fade,
In every drop, sweet dreams are made,
And twilight whispers, soft and sweet,
Guide barefoot dancers on their feet.

So let us raise our cups to cheer,
For citrus charms that bring us near,
In every cloud, a silver line,
The splashing fragrance, pure divine.

Mermaids' Lullaby in Orchard Groves

Amidst the groves where shadows sway,
The mermaids sing at close of day,
Their voices weave through citrus trees,
In harmony with scents and breeze.

With every note, a pearly wave,
The earth below begins to crave,
The stories told in silken dreams,
Where wonders dwell and magic gleams.

The moonlight spills like honeyed dew,
As golden fruits hold secrets true,
While roots entwine in silent glee,
Beneath the waves, they're wild and free.

In twilight's hush, the whispers glide,
Through orchard paths, the spirits bide,
And with each lullaby's embrace,
They brighten up this tranquil space.

So linger here, where night is deep,
As mermaids sing their calming sleep,
In every grove, a story flows,
In harmony with citrus rows.

Enchanted Citrus Currents

Through verdant fields, the breezes sweep,
Where citrus fruits in silence creep,
The currents pull the petals fine,
In secret paths, the low vines twine.

A shimmering rush, a lively dance,
Elixirs born from nature's chance,
They swirl like dreams in twilight's grace,
With secrets held in every space.

In every grove, the laughter rings,
As golden orbs bestow their springs,
With zestful joy, they flow and surge,
Bearing tales where spirits urge.

The air is sweet with citrus bliss,
Each petal touched by nature's kiss,
And as the night begins to fall,
The enchanted citrus calls us all.

So let us wander, hearts in flight,
Through glowing paths of pure delight,
In every breath, a dream ignites,
In currents bright of citrus sights.

Luminous Zest in Deep Waters

Beneath the waves, where shadows play,
Lies zestful life in bright array,
With every bubble, citrus dreams,
Awakened by the moon's soft beams.

The ocean swirls with fragrant tides,
Where lemon fish and lime shells glide,
In phosphorescence, secrets gleam,
Reflecting all that we can't deem.

In currents deep, the treasures hide,
A dance of color, a flowing ride,
With every crest, the spirit soars,
Exploring depths where wonder roars.

The salty breeze sings out a tune,
Invoking dreams beneath the moon,
As citrus blossoms scent the night,
A luminous path that feels so right.

So join the dance where echoes play,
In waters deep, let worries sway,
For zest awaits in every wave,
A world renewed, a heart to save.

Citrus Chrysalis in Aquatic Stillness

In shadows where the waters gleam,
A chrysalis drifts on a silver beam.
Bright oranges and yellows sway,
In the calm, they dance and play.

Beneath the waves, they softly spin,
A world of wonder held within.
Whispers float in liquid air,
Secret dreams beyond compare.

The currents weave a silent song,
Where time flows gently, ever strong.
Each citrus hue a treasured gift,
In stillness, hearts and spirits lift.

With each breath, the colors bloom,
Casting light to banish gloom.
In this realm, a tale untold,
Of secrets kept in shades of gold.

So let us drift in waters clear,
Where each moment brings us near.
Citrus blossoms in quiet grace,
Unfolding dreams in this sacred place.

Secrets of the Aquatic Orchard

In an orchard deep beneath the tide,
Where mysteries and dreams abide,
Citrus fruits in coral shades,
Their sweetness in the twilight fades.

Submerged beneath the emerald hue,
Secrets hidden, old and new.
With every wave, a tale unwinds,
Of ancient wisdom still confined.

Beneath the surface, colors gleam,
A world alive, a whispered dream.
Each fruit a story, ripe with lore,
A treasure waiting to explore.

The currents stream with gentle grace,
Carrying scents to this sacred place.
With every glance, the heart can see,
The secrets shared within the sea.

So dive into the depths of thought,
Where every lesson must be sought.
In each citrus, a truth to find,
Binding us, heart and mind.

The Siren's Citrus Carousel

In twilight hours where shadows cast,
The siren sings, her voice a blast.
Around her swirls a citrus ride,
A carousel of dreams set wide.

Each fruit spins bright on ocean's reel,
A dance of colors, life so real.
Voices echo through the deep,
In rhythms that the waters keep.

With every turn, the flavors blend,
A journey where the lost can mend.
Lemons twirl and limes take flight,
In siren's glow, the world feels right.

So come, dear friend, take heed and spin,
Let citrus wonders draw you in.
The waters whisper, soft and sweet,
The siren's song, a wondrous treat.

In laughter and joy, the ride begins,
With every drop, the courage wins.
Beneath the waves, our spirits soar,
On the citrus carousel forevermore.

Unfurling Citrus Petals in Deep Waters

In the deep where shadows play,
Citrus petals drift and sway.
Unfurling treasures, bright and rare,
In depths of blue, they linger there.

With gentle grace, they rise and fall,
A vibrant dance for one and all.
Lemons, oranges, deeply spun,
In a watery waltz, their journey's begun.

The bubbles rise, a soft embrace,
Citrus dreams in fluid space.
Beneath the light, colors collide,
Each petal's tale a joyful ride.

In this realm, the heart finds peace,
Where worries fade and sorrows cease.
The petals whisper stories old,
In currents warm, their hearts unfold.

So linger long in waters deep,
Where citrus dreams have come to sleep.
In gentle swirls, we've come to know,
The magic in the ebb and flow.

Vibrant Currents of Sour and Sweet

In the garden where flavors mix,
Lemon trees sigh with age-old tricks.
Under the sun's embracing light,
Sweetness dances, a wondrous sight.

Beneath the shade of emerald leaves,
Mysteries hide where nobody believes.
Sour whispers tease the fragrant air,
Inviting hearts to stop and stare.

Rivers of zest flow through the glade,
Where joyous laughter can't evade.
Every drop a memory spun,
Chasing shadows as the day is done.

In the twilight when colors blend,
Nature's secret songs ascend.
With vibrant hues both bright and stark,
A splash of magic lights the dark.

The Citrus Waltz in Midnight Waters

When the moon spills silver on the sea,
Lemons twirl in sweet jubilee.
In quiet waves, the secrets sway,
Dancing softly till break of day.

Rippling currents, a melodious tune,
Every splash a bright festoon.
Citrus dreams beneath the stars,
Whispered tales from distant shores.

Glimmers of gold ride on the tide,
Where playful shadows gently glide.
Fruits of the night sing out their song,
In the waltz of water, all belong.

With each motion, the world feels light,
Bathed in laughter and pure delight.
A moment captured in the breeze,
The citrus waltz beneath the trees.

Forbidden Orchard of the Deep

In the depths where whispers dwell,
An orchard blooms, a secret spell.
Lemon branches twist and turn,
In shadows deep, bright candles burn.

Guarded by the creatures of night,
Sour fruits sparkle, a captivating sight.
Each bite a risk, tantalizingly sweet,
In the forbidden, all dreamers meet.

Leaves rustle with tales untold,
Sunkissed paths lead to treasures bold.
The air is thick with perfumed sighs,
Where fruit and magic intertwine and rise.

Silence sings in hushed delight,
As moonbeams weave through the twilight.
A daring heart shall taste and roam,
In the orchard that calls them home.

Mystical Waves of Lemon's Light

In the realm where daylight shines,
Lemon's glow transcends the pines.
Mystical waves weave tales anew,
Binding earth in colors true.

Ripples carry a fragrant song,
Soft as whispers, wild and strong.
Golden hues upon the sea,
A dance of light, forever free.

With each crest, the world aligns,
In citrus dreams, the heart entwines.
Beneath the sun, beneath the stars,
Nature's magic, forever ours.

Lost in wonder, we drift and sway,
Caught in the moment, we long to stay.
In every wave, in every sight,
The mystical glow of lemon's light.

Zestful Embrace of the Ocean's Whisper

Beneath the sky of azure gleam,
Waves dance with laughter, swift and free.
A wondrous world, where shadows beam,
Embracing dreams, as you and me.

The salty breeze, a tender kiss,
It weaves through locks like silk so fine.
In every hush, I feel the bliss,
The ocean's heart begins to shine.

Barnacles cling on time's embrace,
A story spun with strands of gold.
With every splash, we find our place,
In seas of secrets, brave and bold.

Oh, swirling tides, enchant our fate,
With whispers wrapped in sunlit rays.
We dance along, the world so great,
In gentle waves, our worries sway.

Each sunset dips in colors bright,
A canvas brushed with dreams untold.
The ocean's voice, our guiding light,
Forever young, forever old.

Gilded Treasures in Aquatic Dreams

In depths where sunlight softly falls,
Gold coins shimmer, lost to time.
Once sailors' hoard, now silent calls,
Adrift in waves, a whispered rhyme.

Beneath the soft, embracing tide,
A treasure chest of sea-borne lore.
With every pearl, the heart's pride,
We chase the echoes on the shore.

Each grain of sand, a story's kiss,
Of tempest dreams and starlit seas.
In fleeting moments, find your bliss,
For the ocean's heart holds mysteries.

The shipwrecks tangled in seaweed strands,
Guard tales of hearts, both brave and bold.
With maps that drift on whispering sands,
A path to secrets yet unrolled.

So dive into the deep blue night,
Let gilded dreams adorn your way.
In aquatic realms of pure delight,
Your spirit sails, come what may.

Tangy Secrets of Tidal Shadows

When evening casts its gentle spell,
And shadows play on silver sand,
The ocean stirs, begins to tell,
Of tangy secrets, hand in hand.

Drifting mists that kiss the shore,
Citrus scents that rise with glee.
In every wave, my spirits soar,
With tidal whispers, wild and free.

Shells of treasure hide their song,
In twilight's grasp, their tales unfold.
With tides that ebb, we drift along,
To find the truths the night has told.

The moonbeams dance on crests of foam,
A trail of silver leads the way.
With every crest, we find a home,
In tidal secrets, night and day.

So linger here, where shadows dwell,
And let the ocean's pulse be known.
In every splash, I hear the swell,
Of whispers sweet, forever sown.

The Citrus Serenade of Sirens

In twilight's glow, the sirens sing,
With voices ripe as citrus bloom.
Their melodies, like breezes fling,
A sweetness found in ocean's gloom.

Among the rocks where shadows play,
They lure the ships with songs so bright.
Oh, fragile hearts, let not delay,
For with their tunes, you'll take to flight.

Each note a kiss from ocean's breath,
A citrus blend of joy and woe.
In tides of time, they dance with death,
Yet in their charm, the world will glow.

With laughter light as summer's rays,
They weave their tales through salty air.
A serenade that gently sways,
Entwined in dreams laid soft and rare.

So listen close, let spirits rise,
For every song hides worlds unseen.
Within their harmonies, the skies,
Unravel secrets dipped in green.

Limes in the Luminous Deep

Within the waves, a lime so bright,
Dancing in the moon's soft light.
Echoes of laughter, sweet and clear,
Whispering secrets for all to hear.

Fishes dart in emerald hues,
In this world where magic brews.
A sparkling sea of vivid green,
Where dreams and limes twirl and preen.

The currents sing, a gentle hum,
As the tide brings forth a tale to come.
With every splash, a story spun,
In the deep where wonders run.

Bubbles rise like wishes made,
Frothy dreams in this ocean glade.
Bright citrine drops on coral beds,
Where starry thoughts and sea-life spread.

So take a sip from nature's brew,
Beneath the waves, adventures new.
In the luminous deep, we find our flight,
With limes in hand, our spirits ignite.

Beneath Tangy Tides

Beneath the tides, a treasure lies,
Wrapped in hues of azure skies.
Murmurs of limes and tales of cheer,
Dance on waves, drawing us near.

Citrus scents in salty air,
Fill our lungs, banish despair.
Fish twirl under sunlight's embrace,
In this underwater, vibrant space.

Mirrored surfaces reflect our dreams,
Flowing like laughter in gentle streams.
Bubbles wander like fleeting thoughts,
Nestled where the ocean sways and knots.

Jellyfish glow like lanterns bright,
Guiding souls through the endless night.
Every swirl and every twirl,
Crafts a song in the water's whirl.

As we dive into this sea of zest,
We gather hope, we are truly blessed.
Beneath tangy tides, our hearts shall soar,
Embracing the magic forevermore.

Lemonade Fantasies Under the Sea

In depths where sunbeams softly weave,
Lemonade dreams begin to cleave.
Golden ripples, laughter flows,
In secret nooks where magic grows.

Squid and dolphins play and spin,
In this land where smiles begin.
Joyful spirits in every swell,
Casting spells where stories dwell.

With a splash, the colors blend,
A twist of fate, they never end.
Here, hearts frolic, we find delight,
In every shard of shimmering light.

Seahorses sway in gentle tune,
Beneath the soft and watchful moon.
A fizzy swirl in salty air,
Invites us to join this vibrant fair.

Let waves of lemonade lift our dreams,
In bubbles that burst with joyful beams.
Under the sea, we carve our path,
To a world of laughter and gentle wrath.

Celestial Citrus and Aquatic Dreams

Celestial citrus under the wave,
A world of charm, where souls are brave.
Golden orbs in a sapphire fold,
Whisper tales of treasures untold.

Aquatic realms where the quiet hum,
Calls forth the ancients, a rhythmic drum.
In vibrant patches of coral light,
We weave our dreams, taking flight.

The tide's embrace, a soft caress,
In this haven, we find our rest.
Magic dances on the breeze,
Where waves grant wishes and hearts appease.

Swirling colors upon the sand,
Invite us into this dreamland.
From limes to lemons, a citrus glow,
In the sea's embrace, our spirits grow.

Celestial whispers, aquatic grace,
Entwine our hearts in this sacred space.
With every ripple, our hopes arise,
In dreams of citrus beneath the skies.

The Ocean's Fruitful Melancholy

Waves whisper tales of lost delight,
Where shadows dance beneath the light.
Siren songs weave through the foam,
In depths where ancient spirits roam.

Lonesome hearts upon the shore,
Yearn for what they've known before.
With every tide that ebbs away,
Melancholy drifts to sway.

Pearls of wisdom in the deep,
Secrets that the wavy keep.
But even in the bitter rain,
Beauty blooms amidst the pain.

Fishermen cast their nets anew,
Hoping for a brighter view.
Yet in the catch, a fleeting taste,
Of memories they cannot waste.

So listen close to ocean's sigh,
And let your dreams take wing and fly.
For in each wave, and every tear,
The ocean's heart beats ever near.

Sunkissed Citrus in Siren's Wake

Lemon light on ocean's crest,
Sunkissed fruit, the sea's behest.
Golden glimmers on the tide,
Secrets paired with ocean's pride.

Breezes steal the zest and spice,
Crafting dreams, oh so precise.
Siren's laughter, sweet and bright,
Guides the sailor home tonight.

Citrus glows against the blue,
Every slice tells tales anew.
With every wave that crashes high,
And every breath, the spirit sighs.

Barrels filled with joy, they roll,
Across the sand, they find their goal.
Yet in the mist where secrets lay,
Lemon dreams keep fears at bay.

So taste the sun, embrace the sea,
Let your heart dance wild and free.
In this world of ripe delight,
Sunkissed citrus shines so bright.

Vibrant Flavors of the Deep

In the depths, colors collide,
With vibrant flavors, the ocean cried.
Beneath the waves, a banquet spread,
Where all the tales of twilight bled.

Crimson corals sway and gleam,
In a world adorned in dreams.
Tangled weeds and treasures lost,
Whisper stories of the cost.

Bubbles rise like fleeting thoughts,
Gathering the echoes sought.
Anemones dance, shifting light,
In the embrace of endless night.

Every creature knows its song,
In harmony, they'll all belong.
With every ripple, feelings flare,
In vibrant flavors, love's laid bare.

So taste the sea, let flavors bloom,
For every heart, there's space and room.
In depths where secrets softly weep,
Awakens joy, the flavors deep.

Tidal Loom of Lemon Dreams

Tides weave tales in yellow strands,
Lemon whispers drift on sands.
Underneath the twilight sky,
Dreams take flight, and souls can fly.

Netting hope from ocean's flow,
Each wave reveals what we don't know.
Winds of citrus lift our sails,
Guiding hearts through tempest gales.

With every turn of moonlit tide,
Lemon dreams shall be our guide.
In the tapestry of night,
Stars align, and futures bright.

Kissed by sun, embraced by sea,
We find the place that sets us free.
For in the loom, our stories blend,
Woven tightly, they transcend.

So gather 'round, let laughter ring,
In tidal loops, our spirits sing.
Lemon dreams upon the crest,
In the ocean, we find rest.

Citrus Crescendo in the Abyss

Deep in the abyss where shadows play,
Citrus notes whisper, night turns to day.
Lemons and limes in the tangled sea,
Their zesty embrace calls out to me.

Beneath the waves, where sunlight dips,
Mingling flavors on golden lips.
Tangerines twirl in a dance divine,
Each juicy slice, a treasure to find.

Emerald kelp sways in the current's song,
As the citrus bloom drifts, bright and strong.
Fruits of the ocean, vibrant and bold,
Stories of sweetness waiting to be told.

In the deep water, the chorus unfolds,
With every wave, a tale is retold.
Citrus crescendo, where darkness yields,
To the radiant light that the sea reveals.

The Orange Lull of the Ocean Floor

Beneath the surface, where quiet sleeps,
An orange lull, the ocean keeps.
Crimson corals, softly swaying,
In their warmth, the secrets laying.

Gentle waves cradle all in their fold,
Sandy treasures and stories of old.
A citrus magic that gently lingers,
Call of the sea, with beckoning fingers.

Starfish woven in citrus dreams,
As sunbeams dance on glimmering streams.
Orange hues kiss the ocean's grace,
In the depths, a soft embrace.

While creatures murmur in hushed delight,
Breathless echoes of day and night.
The ocean's lull, a soothing balm,
Nature's whisper, sweet and calm.

Misty Gardens of Tangy Treasures

In misty gardens where flavors ignite,
Tangy treasures bathe in the light.
Mandarin blossoms in blossom abound,
Their fragrant whispers keep joy unbound.

Veils of fog weave an intricate tale,
While dew-kissed fruits in sweetness prevail.
A spark of zest in the morning air,
Hints of sunshine, so vivid and rare.

Lively oranges hang from emerald vines,
Every petal a secret, each branch intertwines.
The garden awakens in fragrant embrace,
A symphony played in a wondrous place.

With every rustle of leaves on the breeze,
The garden smiles, inviting with ease.
In patches of sunlight, where dreams take flight,
Misty gardens hold treasures so bright.

Sirens of Citrus and Salty Breezes

Amidst the tides, where the sirens sing,
Citrus comes forth on the wings of spring.
Sunkissed oranges, bright as the sun,
In salty breezes, they frolic and run.

Calls from the shore, hauntingly sweet,
Echo the oranges, destined to meet.
With fragrant whispers, they guide the way,
Into the heart of a sunlit day.

Salty laughter dances on the waves,
As citrus dreams weave through sun-kissed caves.
A melody of zest in the ocean's embrace,
Every note crafted in nature's grace.

In the twilight glow, as shadows blend,
The sirens of citrus and sea never end.
Together they sing, a song so clear,
A bond of the ocean, forever near.

Luscious Fruits of Twilight Waves

As dusk falls softly, ocean sighs,
Golden fruits gleam under twilight skies.
Whispers of flavor in the gentle breeze,
Nature's sweet bounty, sure to please.

Ripened nectar, colors entwined,
Each bite a treasure, perfectly aligned.
Mangoes and cherries, shimmering bright,
Dancing together in fading light.

The waves bring tales from far away,
Of sun-kissed shores where children play.
In every droplet, secrets abide,
A lush garden where dreams reside.

Birds of paradise sing their tune,
Under the watch of a silver moon.
With each sweet morsel, stories unfold,
Of summer's glory, daring and bold.

So gather around, let laughter grow,
Under the stars with a warm, gentle glow.
Luscious fruits beckon, a feast to share,
In this twilight moment, joys laid bare.

Beneath the Citrus Fog

In mornings hazy, citrus dreams rise,
Fragrant mist dances, veiling the skies.
Lemon drops twinkle like stars on the sea,
A soft, golden glow, inviting and free.

Underneath branches, shadows do play,
With whispers of oranges, sweetened by day.
Grapefruit glimmers, a jewel in the light,
Bursting with flavors, a pure, sheer delight.

In gentle embrace, the fog lingers on,
As tendrils of warmth greet the dawn's song.
Beneath blooming boughs, laughter takes flight,
In a tapestry woven of joy and of light.

Each zesty bite, a burst of the sun,
As nature's wild orchestra begins to run.
With nectar of life in the air, oh so sweet,
Beneath the citrus, find solace complete.

So linger a while where the worlds intertwine,
In the citrus fog, let your spirit align.
For within every breath, a story is spun,
Beneath the bright citrus, where hearts are as one.

A Tidal Symphony of Flavor

The sea's sweet melody calls from afar,
A tidal symphony like a shining star.
Fruits of the ocean, bursting with zest,
In nature's grand concert, they all do their best.

Salty waves frolic, mixing the sweet,
Tangerine whispers on the shore greet.
Seafoam dances like a delicate lace,
In this vibrant world, every taste finds its place.

With every tide, new flavors emerge,
Coconut and lime in a playful surge.
The crash of the waves sets a rhythmic beat,
A celebration of life, both savory and sweet.

Under starry blankets where secrets reside,
The fruits of the tide and the sea take a ride.
Beneath moonlit skies, the magic ignites,
As palates awaken to culinary delights.

So raise up your glass, let joy take the lead,
In this tidal symphony, love is the seed.
For in every flavor, a story is found,
A dance of the sea, where connection is crowned.

Embrace of Citrus and Seafoam

Amidst the waves, where dreams softly blend,
Citrus and seafoam in harmony send.
A gentle caress, as afternoon wanes,
Whispers of fruit in the ocean's refrains.

Limes twist and turn in the salty embrace,
Kissed by the sun, in a warm, loving space.
Each droplet of flavor dances, alive,
Inviting the spirit to joyfully thrive.

Under pale skies, the twilight unfolds,
With oranges glimmering like rays that are gold.
The sea sings its song, while time drifts away,
In the cradle of nature, forever to stay.

With laughter and beauty, the moments are spun,
Where seafoam and citrus create one.
In every wave's lift, in every sweet bite,
An embrace of the elements, tender and bright.

So gather your heart, let your spirit take flight,
In the citrusy calm of a warm summer night.
For in this embrace, all worries will cease,
In the magic of flavor, the soul finds its peace.

Orchard Dreams

In twilight's arms, the blossoms sway,
Whispers of green blend sweet and gray.
Each petal tells a story, forlorn,
Of sunlit days and the promise of dawn.

A breeze caresses the fruit-filled trees,
A dance of shadows, a soft, sweet breeze.
Beneath the boughs, where secrets lie,
Dreams gather close and silently sigh.

The apples blush and the pears gleam bright,
Each drop of dew, a star in the night.
In hidden nooks, where the fairies play,
Orchard dreams blossom and drift away.

With every bud, a wish takes flight,
In this enchanted, profound delight.
The ground beneath, alive with sound,
Holds echoes of magic, forever bound.

As daylight fades, the colors blend,
In the orchard's heart, where magic won't end.
Under the moon's watchful gaze,
Dreams and fruits weave a timeless maze.

Siren's Songs

In foam and mist, the sirens weep,
Their haunting calls, a promise deep.
With each soft note, the waters churn,
Luring sailors with secrets to learn.

Beneath the waves where shadows glide,
They weave their lore, with the tide as guide.
Enticing hearts with tales of old,
Of treasure and love, of dreams to behold.

Stars flicker bright in the deepening blue,
As shimmering scales dance into view.
A lullaby echoes through night's embrace,
Where currents sing in a wistful place.

Yet danger lurks, with its tempting lies,
For not all beats end in soft goodbyes.
With each sweet song, a choice we face,
To follow our hearts or win the race.

So heed the whispers that drift in the breeze,
For siren songs travel with such ease.
In their melody, the sea finds her voice,
A riddle to ponder, a haunting choice.

Splashes of Zing in the Blue Horizon

Upon the canvas of endless blue,
Zestful splashes of color break through.
With laughter and joy, the sunlight gleams,
Bringing to life our wildest dreams.

The waves toss bright shades on the shore,
Each ripple a memory, a vibrant lore.
Bubbles of laughter ride the air,
Tickling the senses, beyond compare.

Sandcastles rise under a playful sun,
Time slows down and all worries are spun.
Children frolic with hearts full of cheer,
While vibrant shells whisper stories near.

As the day fades to a soft pastel,
The horizon glows, casting its spell.
With hues that inspire and spirits that sing,
In the twilight glow, we find our wing.

The world may turn, but here we'll stay,
In splashes of zing, where dreams come to play.
Embracing the beauty in every view,
We dance on the shoreline, just me and you.

The Hidden Dance of Lime and Sea

In shades of green where limes do grow,
The salty sea whispers soft and low.
A fusion of flavors, a melody sweet,
Where citrus mingles with each wave's beat.

Each gust of wind brings tales from afar,
Of distant lands and the evening star.
In hidden corners, where secrets blend,
Lime and sea conspire, the world they mend.

With every splash, the dance ignites,
A rhythm alive under soft moonlight.
From beaches warm to cool, dark depths,
Nature's ballet in secret sweeps and inept.

The tide retreats, yet leaves its trace,
A canvas untouched, a sacred space.
In the heart of the wild, tranquility waits,
As the limes twirl with fate—the sea elates.

So let us wander where the dancers play,
In hidden glades where the flowers sway.
With spirits entwined and laughter so free,
We'll uncover the dance of lime and sea.

Driftwood and Dill

Along the shore where time takes pause,
Driftwood lies, nature's old applause.
Twisted forms tell tales from the past,
Of storms and calm, of moments vast.

Beside it grows the fragrant dill,
A sprig of green on the window sill.
Its scent dances in the soft, warm air,
Inviting dreams of comfort to share.

The waves crash gently against the wood,
In harmony, where nature has stood.
Each piece a journey, a story untold,
Waves whisper secrets, both new and old.

With every breeze, there's magic on hand,
As the driftwood anchors in soft, warm sand.
Dill sways lightly, a graceful embrace,
In this tranquil haven, we find our place.

Let time meander as the sun takes flight,
In driftwood and dill, all feels just right.
Together we wander, hand in hand we'll stow,
The stories of old, where the wild winds blow.

Shimmering Tides

In the quietude of the moonlit night,
Tides shimmer softly, a silvery sight.
They draw the heart to the edge of the shore,
With whispers of magic that beckon for more.

Waves crest and tumble, a glistening dance,
Under starlit skies, they twirl in a trance.
Each splash is a promise, each swell is a kiss,
A moment of wonder, pure ocean bliss.

With grains of sand that sparkle like gold,
Secrets are kept, and stories unfold.
In the salty air, dreams drift away,
As night weaves its tapestry, soft and gray.

The tides rock gently, a lullaby sweet,
Where the ocean meets land, our hearts feel complete.
In shimmering light, we lose track of time,
In this world of quiet, our spirits climb.

So let us wander where the water glows,
In the embrace of tides, as the soft wind blows.
For in shimmering tides, we find our dreams,
In the dance of the night and the moon's soft beams.